HomeBuilders *Couples Series* ®

building your mate's
Self-Esteem

MVFOL

By Dennis and Barbara Rainey

"Unless the Lord builds the house, its builders labor in vain"
(Psalm 127:1a).

D1025608

FAMILYLIFE™
Bringing Timeless Principles Home
Little Rock, Arkansas

Group
Loveland, Colorado

Group's R.E.A.L. Guarantee to you:

Every Group resource incorporates our R.E.A.L. approach to ministry—a unique philosophy that results in long-term retention and life transformation. It's ministry that's:

This is EARL.
He's R.E.A.L.
mixed-up.
(Get it?)

Relational
Because student-to-student interaction enhances learning and builds Christian friendships.

Experiential
Because what students experience sticks with them up to 9 times longer than what they simply hear or read.

Applicable
Because the aim of Christian education is to be both hearers and doers of the Word.

Learner-based
Because students learn more and retain it longer when the process is designed according to how they learn best.

Building Your Mate's Self-Esteem

Copyright © 2000 Dennis and Barbara Rainey

Visit our Web site: **www.grouppublishing.com**

Credits
FamilyLife
Editor: David Boehi
Assistant Editor: Julie Denker

Group Publishing, Inc.
Editor: Matt Lockhart
Creative Development Editor: Paul Woods
Chief Creative Officer: Joani Schultz
Copy Editor: Alison Imbriaco
Art Director: Jenette L. McEntire
Cover Art Director: Jeff A. Storm
Computer Graphic Artist: Anita M. Cook
Cover Photographer: FPG International
Illustrators: Ken Jacobsen, Dana Regan
Production Manager: Peggy Naylor

ISBN 0-7644-2235-9
10 9 8 7 6   09 08 07 06 05 04 03

Printed in the United States of America.

How to Let the Lord Build Your House
and not labor in vain

●

The HomeBuilders Couples Series®: A small-group Bible study dedicated to making your family all that God intended.

FamilyLife is a division of Campus Crusade for Christ International, an evangelical Christian organization founded in 1951 by Bill Bright. FamilyLife was started in 1976 to help fulfill the Great Commission by strengthening marriages and families and then equipping them to go to the world with the gospel of Jesus Christ. The FamilyLife Marriage Conference is held in most major cities throughout the United States and is one of the fastest-growing marriage conferences in America today. "FamilyLife Today," a daily radio program hosted by Dennis Rainey, is heard on hundreds of stations across the country. Information on all resources offered by FamilyLife may be obtained by contacting us at the address, telephone number, or World Wide Web site listed below.

Dennis Rainey, Executive Director
FamilyLife
P.O. Box 8220
Little Rock, AR 72221-8220
1-800-FL-TODAY
www.familylife.com

A division of Campus Crusade for Christ International
Bill Bright, Founder and President

About the Sessions

Each session in this study is composed of the following categories: Warm-Up, Blueprints, Wrap-Up, and HomeBuilders Project. A description of each of these categories follows:

Warm-Up (15 minutes)

The purpose of Warm-Up is to help people unwind from a busy day and get to know each other better. Typically the first point in Warm-Up is an exercise that is meant to be fun while introducing the topic of the session. The ability to share in fun with others is important in building relationships. Another component of Warm-Up is the Project Report (except in Session One), which is designed to provide accountability for the HomeBuilders Project that is to be completed by couples between sessions.

Blueprints (60 minutes)

This is the heart of the study. In this part of each session, people answer questions related to the topic of study and look to God's Word for understanding. Some of the questions are to be answered by couples, in subgroups, or in the group at large. There are notes in the margin or instructions within a question that designate these groupings.

Wrap-Up (15 minutes)

This category serves to "bring home the point" and wind down a session in an appropriate fashion.

HomeBuilders Project (60 minutes)

This project is the unique application step in a HomeBuilders study. Before leaving a meeting, couples are encouraged to "Make a Date" to do this project prior to the next meeting. Each HomeBuilders Project contains three sections: 1) As a Couple—a brief exercise designed to get the date started in a fun way; 2) Individually—a section of questions for husbands and wives to answer separately; 3) Interact as a Couple—an opportunity for couples to share their answers with each other and to make application in their lives.

In addition to the above regular features, occasional activities are labeled "For Extra Impact." These are activities that generally provide a more active or visual way to make a particular point. Be mindful that people within a group have different learning styles. While most of what is presented is verbal, a visual or active exercise now and then helps engage more of the senses and appeals to people who learn best by seeing, touching, and doing.

About the Authors

Dennis Rainey is the executive director and the cofounder of FamilyLife (a division of Campus Crusade for Christ) and a graduate of Dallas Theological Seminary. Since 1976, he has overseen the rapid growth of FamilyLife Conferences on marriage and parenting. He is also the daily host of the nationally syndicated radio program, "FamilyLife Today."

Dennis and his wife, Barbara, have spoken at FamilyLife Conferences across the United States and overseas. Dennis is also a speaker for Promise Keepers. He has testified on family issues before Congress and has appeared on numerous radio and television programs.

Dennis and Barbara have co-authored several books, including, *Building Your Mate's Self-Esteem* (re-released as *The New Building Your Mate's Self-Esteem*), *Moments Together for Couples, Parenting Today's Adolescent,* and *Starting Your Marriage Right.*

Dennis and Barbara have served on the staff of Campus Crusade since 1971. They have six children and one grandchild. They are both graduates of the University of Arkansas and live near Little Rock, Arkansas.

Contents

Acknowledgments

We first want to express special thanks to two individuals who played key roles when this study was first written.

To Jeff Tikson, the best utility infielder we've seen: You helped hatch this idea years ago and played a key role in seeing this whole HomeBuilders Couples Series become a reality. You coached, encouraged, asked tough questions, and helped sharpen this material immeasurably. Thanks, not only for the hours you spent serving us on this project (so we could complete it), but for your enduring friendship as well. God has great things in store for you in the days ahead.

Hard work and a heart for people are synonyms for Jerry Wunder. Thanks, Jerry, for pushing us and this project along. You know that because of the leadership role you've played in FamilyLife, you've given us the precious commodity of time— time to write, create, sharpen, and give birth to this small-group study. It wouldn't have happened if you hadn't come to join our team when you did.

In addition, we want to thank Dave Boehi, as well as Matt Lockhart and Paul Woods at Group Publishing, for their work in revising this material.

Finally, if you don't know Julie Denker, you should. She's got a great grin and a tenacious spirit. If you don't think so, just try a game of basketball or slow-pitch softball with her. She has been the steady plodder of the HomeBuilders Couples Series from its inception. Julie, our deepest gratitude goes to you for the hundreds of hours you spent editing and tracking this project. It is to you that this book is dedicated.

Introduction

When a man and woman are married, they stand before a room of witnesses and proclaim their commitment to a lifetime of love. They recite a sacred vow "to have and to hold...from this day forward...to love, honor, and cherish...for better, for worse...for richer, for poorer...in sickness and in health...as long as we both shall live."

It's a happy day, perhaps the happiest in their lives. And yet, once the honeymoon ends, once the emotions of courtship and engagement subside, many couples realize that "falling in love" and building a good marriage are two different things. Keeping those vows is much more difficult than they thought it would be.

Otherwise intelligent people, who would not think of buying a car, investing money, or even going to the grocery store without some initial planning, enter into marriage with no plan of how to make that relationship succeed.

But God has already provided the plan, a set of blueprints for building a truly God-honoring marriage. His plan is designed to enable a man and woman to grow together in a mutually satisfying relationship and then to reach out to others with the love of Christ. Ignoring this plan leads only to isolation and separation between husband and wife. It's a pattern evident in so many homes today: Failure to follow God's blueprints results in wasted effort, bitter disappointment, and, in far too many cases, divorce.

In response to this need in marriages today, FamilyLife has developed a series of small-group studies called the HomeBuilders Couples Series.

You could complete this study alone with your spouse, but we strongly urge you to either form or join a group of couples studying this material. You will find that the questions in each session not only help you grow closer to your spouse, but they help create a special environment of warmth and fellowship as you study together how to build the type of marriage you desire. Participating in a HomeBuilders group could be one of the highlights of your married life.

The Bible: Your Blueprints for a God-Honoring Marriage

You will notice as you proceed through this study that the Bible is used frequently as the final authority on issues of life and marriage. Although written thousands of years ago, this Book still speaks clearly and powerfully about the conflicts and struggles faced by men and women. The Bible is God's Word— his blueprints for building a God-honoring home and for dealing with the practical issues of living.

We encourage you to have a Bible with you for each session. For this series we use the New International Version as our primary reference. Another excellent translation is the New American Standard Bible.

Ground Rules

Each group session is designed to be enjoyable and informative—and nonthreatening. Three simple ground rules will help ensure that everyone feels comfortable and gets the most out of the experience:

1. Don't share anything that would embarrass your spouse.

2. You may pass on any question you don't want to answer.

3. If possible, plan to complete the HomeBuilders Project as a couple between group sessions.

A Few Quick Notes About Leading a HomeBuilders Group

1. Leading a group is much easier than you may think! A group leader in a HomeBuilders session is really a "facilitator." As a leader, your goal is simply to guide the group through the discussion questions. You don't need to teach the material—in fact, we don't want you to! The special dynamic of a HomeBuilders group is that couples teach themselves.

2. This material is designed to be used in a home study, but it also can be adapted for use in a Sunday school environment. (See page 121 for more information about this option.)

3. We have included a section of Leader's Notes in the back of this book. Be sure to read through these notes before leading a session; they will help you prepare.

4. For more material on leading a HomeBuilders group, be sure to get a copy of the *HomeBuilders Leader Guide*, by Drew and Kit Coons. This book is an excellent resource that provides helpful guidelines on how to start a study, how to keep discussion moving, and much more.

Recommended Reading
To enhance your HomeBuilders experience, we recommend reading Dennis and Barbara Rainey's book, *The New Building Your Mate's Self-Esteem* (Thomas Nelson 1995). This book provides further material on the topics discussed in this study.

A Word About Self-Esteem

The subject of self-esteem strikes some Christians negatively. While we must be careful how we approach this subject, self-esteem itself is biblical.

We believe God wants us to realize what we are—children of God. The focus of this study is not on your "self," but on your spouse's self-esteem. Thus, the need we address in our book, *The New Building Your Mate's Self-Esteem,* and in this HomeBuilders study is not how to manipulate your mate to build you up but how to help your mate realize who he or she is as a child of God. Perhaps a good subtitle to our book and to this study would be, "How to Minister to Your Mate." In these pages you will find practical ways to build up, strengthen, and encourage your mate.

It is our hope that your marriage will benefit from this study and from the accountability it provides. May you be successful in building up one another and in building your home.

Strengthening Self-Esteem

Marriage provides one of life's best relationships
for building another's self-esteem.

W A R M • U P   15   M I N U T E S

The Day We Wed

Take turns introducing yourselves and answering one
of the following questions about the day you were
married:

- What was the weather like?
- Who traveled the farthest to attend your wedding?
- What special song was sung?
- What happened that you didn't expect?

Getting Connected

Pass your books around the room, and have couples

list their names, phone numbers, and e-mail addresses in the space provided.

_____
NAME, PHONE, & E-MAIL

_____
NAME, PHONE, & E-MAIL

_____
NAME, PHONE, & E-MAIL

_____
NAME, PHONE, & E-MAIL

_____
NAME, PHONE, & E-MAIL

_____
NAME, PHONE, & E-MAIL

BLUEPRINTS   60 MINUTES

The Need

If you have a large group, form smaller groups of about six people to answer the Blueprints questions. Unless otherwise noted, answer the questions in your subgroup. After finishing each section, take time for subgroups to share their answers with the whole group.

1. One of the greatest needs every individual has is to be "built-up"—to be encouraged or strengthened—in the task of living. What are some reasons this is true?

2. How can self-esteem affect a person
- positively?

- negatively?

3. Scripture often exhorts Christians to build one another up. How do you think 1 Thessalonians 5:11 applies to a married couple?

4. A crucial ingredient in any successful marriage is recognition, by both husband and wife, of the importance of building up the other person in the relationship. What are some ways this can be done in a marriage relationship?

5. Form two groups so each group can take one of the following Scripture passages:
- Romans 15:5-7

• Ephesians 4:29-32

Read the passage and discuss how it relates to the building up of one's mate. Then share your verses and insights with the other group.

6. Read Romans 12:3. What added insight about self-esteem do you gain from this verse?

Having examined the need for self-esteem, let's look at one of the major influences on self-esteem.

The Culprit:
Wrong Standards of Comparison

In your mind, you have a picture of how a husband or wife should act. And, chances are, this image is so perfect, so idyllic, that it is *completely unattainable*. Yet, every day you judge your performance by this phantom! And since you cannot match the idyllic standards, your self-esteem suffers. Read the following descriptions of the Phantom Perfect Wife and Phantom Perfect Husband, then answer the questions that follow.

Phantom Perfect Wife

She is always loving, patient, and understanding. She is well organized, with a perfect balance between being disciplined and
flexible. Her house is always neat and well decorated, and her
children obey her every command. She never gets angry with
her children, even when they forget to do their chores. She is
energetic and never tired, even after working all day and getting
up five times during the night to tend her children. She reaches
out to her neighbors and takes meals to the sick and needy. She
looks fresh and attractive at all times, whether relaxing in jeans
and a sweater, digging in the garden, or going out to dinner in a
silk dress. Her hair always does what she wants it to do, and it's
never flat. Her fingernails are never broken. She always plans
healthy, balanced meals for her family and bakes everything
from scratch. She walks faithfully with God every day and studies and memorizes Scripture.

Phantom Perfect Husband

He rises early, has a quiet time reading the Bible and praying,
and then jogs several seven-minute miles. He never forgets to
hug and kiss his wife goodbye before leaving in time to be at
work ten minutes early. He is consistently patient with his co-
workers, always content with his job, and able to devise creative
solutions to problems at any moment. He works hard, never
wastes time, and arrives home from work on time every day. He
is well read in world events, politics, and important social issues. He is a handyman around the house and never turns down
a request to play with his children. He is popular with everyone
he meets and never tires of helping others in their time of need.
He can quote large sections of Scripture in a single bound, has
faith more powerful than a locomotive, and is faster than a
speeding bullet when solving family conflicts. He never gets discouraged, never wants to quit, and always has the right words
for any circumstance. He never loses things, always flosses his
teeth, has no trouble with his weight, and has time to fish.

7. Now take two or three minutes to write down some descriptions of your phantom.

Answer questions 8 and 9 with your mate. After answering, you may want to share an appropriate insight or discovery with the group.

8. Share with your mate what you wrote in response to 7. How did you feel as you wrote down these descriptions?

9. What impact does your phantom have on your self-esteem?

God's Truth: A New Standard

10. By looking to God's Word, we can find out how much worth and value we have to God. Have each couple take one of the following passages. (It's OK for a couple to take more than one passage or for more than one couple to have the same passage depending on the number in your group.)

- Genesis 1:26-29
- Psalm 139:13-16
- Psalm 139:17-18
- Matthew 6:25-26
- Matthew 10:29-31
- John 3:16-17

Read your passage and discuss the truth it contains and how that truth brings value to your mate. Then share your passage and insights with the group.

11. Why are these truths often difficult to grasp on a daily basis?

12. What can you do this week to remain mindful of God's truth and avoid being a victim of your phantom?

HomeBuilders Principle:
As you and your mate discover and understand the value you have to God, as found in Scripture, you can help one another slay your phantoms and become all God wants you to be.

Recap

Close this session with prayer, and make sure couples Make a Date for this session's Home-Builders Project before they leave.

Round One:

On a slip of paper, write a one- or two-word response to complete the following sentence:

• How I felt about coming to this group tonight was _____.

Once everyone is finished, pass the slips of paper to the leader. (Note: Do not sign your paper, your response is to be anonymous.) The leader then will complete the sentence by sharing from the slips of paper.

Round Two:

On a slip of paper, write a one- or two-word response to complete the following sentence:

• How I'm feeling now, after going through this first session, is _____.

Once everyone is finished, pass the slips of paper to the leader. The leader then will complete the sentence by sharing from the slips of paper.

Round Three:

As a group, discuss some ways this group can encourage and support its members over the course of this study.

Make a Date

Make a date with your mate to meet before the next session to complete the HomeBuilders Project. At the next session, your leader will ask you to share one thing from this experience.

_____

DATE

_____

TIME

_____

LOCATION

HOMEBUILDERS PROJECT   6 0   M I N U T E S

As a Couple [5 minutes]

Begin your date by sharing with each other the following two things:

- What was something you were good at in elementary school?

- What was something you were good at in high school?

Now answer the following question for your mate:
- What is something you are good at now?

Individually [20 minutes]

1. Self-Esteem Inventory

Read through the following list of descriptions, then use the letters below to rank how well each description fits you.

<u>U = Usually</u>   <u>S = Sometimes</u>   <u>R = Rarely</u>

Self	Description
_____	fearful of change
_____	fearful of rejection
_____	seeks to identify with accomplishments
_____	critical of self
_____	easily discouraged
_____	preoccupied with past

_____ defensive
_____ driven by performance
_____ seeks identity through position
_____ lacks decisiveness
_____ critical of others
_____ compares self with others
_____ fearful of failure
_____ tends to believe the worst about a situation
_____ can be paralyzed by own inadequacies
_____ seeks identity through accumulation of wealth
_____ has difficulty establishing meaningful relationships
_____ hides weaknesses
_____ attempts to control others to make self look good
_____ seeks identity through association with significant others
_____ overly self-conscious
_____ has unreal expectations of self
_____ needs continual approval
_____ has difficulty opening up

2. Now go back through the descriptions, and put a star next to the two or three you struggle with the most.

3. Look at the list again, and make a note next to the two or three areas you think your mate struggles with the most.

Interact as a Couple [35 minutes]
1. Share with your mate how you evaluated yourself on the Self-Esteem Inventory.

2. How well did you already know where your mate struggles the most with self-esteem? What ranking, if any, surprised you?

3. Discuss one or two ways you could better support each other in the areas in which you struggle.

4. Together read 2 Corinthians 12:9-10. Discuss from this passage how Paul viewed his weaknesses and what application you could make of his view.

5. Read the following personal pledge statement with your mate:

> *"I pledge to you that I will use the next six sessions of this HomeBuilders study to build, strengthen, and encourage our marriage. I will make this study a priority in my schedule by faithfully keeping our dates, working through the projects, and participating in the group discussions."*

(signed) _____

Will you honor your mate by making this pledge your special commitment to him or her? If so, sign this pledge in your mate's book.

6. Close by praying for one another. Thank God for your mate. Ask God to use you to help your mate see who he or she is in his eyes. Ask that your weaknesses be used to demonstrate God's power in your lives.

Remember to bring your calendar to the next session so you can Make a Date.

Unconditional Acceptance

Help your mate experience the liberating power
of unconditional love.

W A R M • U P   15   M I N U T E S

Best Friends

Share with the group your answer to one of the following questions:

- Who was your best friend when you were growing
  up, and what made you close?

- Think about someone who helped you make the
  transition to a new school, job, neighborhood, or
  church. What did that person do that helped
  you the most?

- What's the closest group or team that you've been
  a part of?

Project Report

Share one thing you learned from last session's HomeBuilders Project.

For Extra Impact

Who Are You?
Use this exercise as a fun way to look at the issue of acceptance.
Leader: To make this exercise work, check page 131 of the Leader's Notes. It provides identity descriptions. You'll need to photocopy this list.

To start, have everyone draw a slip of paper that describes a new, fictional identity. Read your description to yourself, and take a minute to think about your new identity. Choose a name for yourself. Ask yourself: How comfortable would this person be in this group? Then take turns going around the group introducing yourselves. After everyone has been introduced, discuss the following questions:

- How did you feel about being the person you were?
- How accepting did you feel of the others in the group?
- What does this exercise illustrate to you about acceptance?

One of the greatest human needs is unconditional love and acceptance. Unfortunately,
the fear of rejection is a controlling influence in many lives and marriages.

A Controlling Influence

1. Read Genesis 3:1-10. What insight about
the fear of rejection do you find in this passage?

If you have a large group, form smaller groups of about six people to answer the Blueprints questions. Unless other-wise noted, answer the questions in your sub-group. After finishing each section, take time for subgroups to share their answers with the whole group.

2. Why do people fear rejection?

3. What are some ways that the fear of rejection can
affect a marriage relationship?

4. In a marriage relationship, what are some ways people try to protect themselves from rejection?

5. Read Ephesians 2:4-7. What do you find in those verses about your ultimate acceptance by God?

> **HomeBuilders Principle:**
> *To experience a healthy marriage, you must strive to totally and unconditionally accept your mate.*

Commitment to Acceptance

6. Read Genesis 2:21-24. What components of acceptance do you see in these verses? How do these verses demonstrate a commitment to acceptance?

Answer questions 7 and 8 with your mate. After answering, you may want to share an appropriate insight or discovery with the group.

7. While it may be true that "opposites attract," it's also true that the differences that first attracted you to your mate can later become sources of aggravation.

BUILDING YOUR MATE'S SELF-ESTEEM

• What are some ways, other than physically, you and your mate are different?

• How have you seen God use these differences in your marriage?

8. What is one way you can demonstrate your commitment to accepting your mate?

Demonstration of Love

As you have probably already discovered, words or acts that communicate love and acceptance to you don't always communicate the same message to your mate. You may have to change the way you convey your message so that your mate can feel loved and accepted.

9. Read 1 Corinthians 13. How do the descriptions of love from this chapter contrast with the way love is commonly portrayed in society, particularly in television, movies, and music? How does this chapter challenge you when it comes to thinking about what love really is?

10. Review the following elements of love taken from verses 4 through 8 of 1 Corinthians 13 and answer the questions that follow. (Answer the questions individually first, then share responses with your mate.)

Love...

is patient	keeps no record of wrongs
is kind	does not delight in evil
does not envy	rejoices with the truth
does not boast	always protects
is not proud	always trusts
is not rude	always hopes
is not self-seeking	always perseveres
is not easily angered	never fails

- From the preceding list, which elements of love do you feel your mate is particularly good at demonstrating? Specifically, what does your mate say or do that makes you feel this way?

• What element of love do you want to express more effectively to your mate? What is one way you could begin to do that?

11. Share one answer to question 10 with the group. (Remember, don't share anything that would embarrass your mate.)

12. Read 1 John 4:18. How does this verse describe the effect of love?

HomeBuilders Principle:
Only as your mate experiences the security of your unconditional love will he or she risk being vulnerable in your marriage relationship.

Form two groups—men and women—and decide which group will take which column of love descriptions from Blueprints question 10. In your groups, brainstorm about ways each of the descriptions in your column could be demonstrated in marriage in a practical way. Keep the focus on ways *you* could demonstrate these traits, not on what you would like to see your mate do for you. After five to ten minutes, stop so groups can report what they came up with. Then close with a minute of silent prayer. During this time, reflect on which of the ideas developed in this exercise you should determine to put into practice in your marriage.

Make a Date

Make a date with your mate to meet before the next session to complete the HomeBuilders Project. Your leader will ask you to share one thing from this experience at the next session.

DATE

TIME

LOCATION

HOMEBUILDERS PROJECT   6 0   M I N U T E S

As a Couple [10 minutes]

Take a minute and record an answer to the following
questions. Then share your answers with each other.

- Back when you were dating, what was one of your
  most creative expressions of your love for your
  (now) mate?

- What was one of your mate's most creative
  expressions of love?

Individually [20 minutes]

1. What is one way your mate expresses love and acceptance to you that you appreciate?

2. In what areas of your life are you feeling confident and accepted right now?

3. In what areas are you fearful or afraid of rejection? How is this affecting you?

4. In what way, if any, might you be making it difficult for your mate to be more transparent?

5. How can you better express to your mate the kind of love that "drives out fear"?

6. How can your mate pray positively for you? List at least three areas.

Interact as a Couple [30 minutes]

1. Share your answers from the individual section with each other.

2. From this session and your discussion of the individual section answers, what is one insight you have gained about your mate?

3. Together read Romans 15:7. How are you doing at accepting one another?

4. Finish by praying positively for each other in the areas you listed individually. Thank God for your mate.

Remember to bring your calendar to the next session so you can Make a Date.

For Extra Impact

Love Note: As a couple, you may want to consider doing this exercise to further communicate and reinforce your commitment to accepting each other.

Write a one- or two-paragraph statement expressing your love for, commitment to, and acceptance of your mate. Be sure to include a statement about casting out fear of rejection. Sign and date it, and deliver it to your mate.

Putting the Past in Perspective

Build hope and gain perspective by understanding what effect the past can have on your mate's self-esteem today.

W A R M • U P   15 M I N U T E S

Down Memory Lane

Share a childhood memory recalled by one of these questions:

- What positive experience—a particular accomplishment, for example, or something someone said about you—can still make you feel good to this day?

- What not-so-positive experience—perhaps an embarrassing moment—can you laugh about today, although the memory still makes you cringe?

After everyone has had a chance to share, take turns answering this question:

In general when you think back to your childhood, how do you feel?

❏ I get butterflies in my stomach, and my palms get sweaty.

❏ I'm glad it's over.

❏ I wish I could do it all over again.

❏ It makes me smile.

❏ Other: _____

Project Report

Share one thing you learned from last session's Home-Builders Project.

For Extra Impact

These Are a Few of My Favorite Things: Use this exercise as a fun way to reflect on your past. (Leader: See note number 3 on p. 134 of Leader's Notes for instructions about this exercise.)

From the various objects, select one that brings a childhood memory to mind. Then answer one or two of the following questions:

• How is this item similar to one of your favorite things as a child?

• When you see and touch this item, how do you feel?

• In what way do you feel one's childhood is still a part of who that person is today?

A Special Message

Even when we don't realize it, past mistakes and wrong choices, including those made by others, can have a profound impact on us today. This session may touch on some sensitive areas from the past. It is not the purpose of this session to embarrass anyone, to reopen old wounds, or to cause anyone to feel guilt for something God has already forgiven. Rather, the intent is that two things occur:

- You recognize the impact the past has had on you for good and bad.
- You learn biblical principles that will help you put the past behind you.

You and your mate can build a relationship in which you lovingly remind each other of God's forgiveness. However, if there is something you and your mate *cannot* work through, we recommend that you ask for help from your pastor or a competent Christian counselor.

Throughout this session—and this HomeBuilders Project— remember to share nothing that would embarrass your mate or that you don't feel safe in sharing.

The Effect of the Past on Self-Esteem

1. How does the past affect self-esteem, both positively and negatively?

If you have a large group, form smaller groups of about six people to answer the Blueprints questions. Unless otherwise noted, answer the questions in your subgroup. After finishing each section, take time for subgroups to share their answers with the whole group.

2. One area of the past that will always affect you is your relationship with your parents. How has this relationship affected your self-esteem...

• positively?

• negatively?

3. For good or bad, how did your peers—friends and siblings—affect your self-esteem when you were growing up?

4. What other individuals had a significant influence on who you are today through their effect on your self-esteem?

5. What we do affects how we feel. Looking to the Bible, we can see an example of this in the life of David.

For question 5, form two groups so that one group can look at 2 Samuel 11 and the other can look at Psalm 51. Read your chapter and answer the related question. Then share your answers with the other group.

- Read 2 Samuel 11. What sins did David commit?

- Read Psalm 51. What sense do you get about how David is feeling? What is David doing?

6. What insights about dealing with the past do you gain from David's example?

HomeBuilders Principle:
To put your pasts behind you and have hope for the future, you and your mate must experience and express God's forgiveness through Jesus Christ.

Encouragement From the Word

7. Read 2 Corinthians 5:17. What unique solution does Christianity offer that affects one's view of past mistakes?

8. Read Isaiah 43:18-19. What encouragement do these verses give you for the future?

9. Although Paul, prior to becoming an apostle, actively persecuted Christians (see Acts 8:3 and 22:4), he was able—through Christ—to put his past behind him. From the writings of Paul, let's look at Scriptures that can help us deal with the past. (Have each couple take one of the following passages.)

- Romans 8:1-2
- Romans 8:37-39
- Ephesians 4:32
- Philippians 3:12-14
- Philippians 4:6-7
- Philippians 4:13

With your mate, read your passage. What hope or encouragement for the future do you find? After answering this question, share with the group your passage and the encouragement you found.

10. Of the verses and insights that were just shared, which do you find most meaningful to you right now? Why?

Helping Your Mate Put the Past in Perspective

While the past provides both positive and negative influences, it is the negative ones that cause us problems in the present. As you and your mate talk about each other's past and attempt to help each other deal with the negative situations, do not overlook the positive influences.

11. We read in Ephesians 4:32 that we are to forgive "just as in Christ God forgave you." Since, by grace, God offers forgiveness to us, how should you and your mate respond to each other's past mistakes?

Answer questions 11 and 12 with your mate. After answering, you may want to share an appropriate insight or discovery with the group.

12. How can you help your mate in "forgetting what is behind" and experience the reality of Philippians 3:13?

HomeBuilders Principle:
When it comes to dealing with the past, you can best help your mate by providing love, acceptance, and forgiveness.

From the following list of positive attributes, pick one that you feel your mate reflects particularly well. Think about an episode from your mate's life that you feel illustrates this attribute, and share it with the group.

- honest
- kind
- generous
- courageous
- talented

- forgiving
- patient
- intelligent
- strong
- humble

Make a Date

Make a date with your mate to meet before the next session to complete the HomeBuilders Project. At the next session, your leader will ask you to share one thing from this experience.

DATE

TIME

LOCATION

Approach this project with caution. Perhaps no area of our lives haunts us more than our past and the mistakes we or others have made. Different marriages have grown to different levels of mature love, acceptance, and trust. The best advice for a project like this is to share what needs to be discussed and put your mate's past behind you. Never pry, and avoid unpleasant details except when it is absolutely necessary to discuss them.

If sensitive areas are exposed as you discuss the past, don't use these "failures" to punish your mate further. Remember: "Perfect love drives out fear" (1 John 4:18).

Note: If you are in doubt about sharing something with your mate, don't do it now. It may be necessary to seek outside counseling if substantial issues arise that cannot be, or should not be, dealt with in this context.

As a Couple [10 minutes]

Start your date by pulling out or describing some special memento from your childhood, perhaps an award, a special toy, or a gift. Even if you have shared this with your mate before, tell your mate the "story" behind your special treasure—when you received it, how old you where, and why it is important to you.

Individually [20 minutes]

For this part of the HomeBuilders Project, you can choose one of three options. Check the box for the option you would like to deal with, then go to the section of this project that describes it. You and your mate may each choose different options. You may want to consider doing the options you didn't select at some later date.

❏ Parents (Option A)

❏ Peers (Option B)

❏ The Past in General (Option C)

Parents (Option A)

1. Describe your home and family when you were growing up. What words come to mind?

2. As parents, what things did your dad and mom do best?

Dad:

Mom:

3. What did they not do well?
Dad:

Mom:

4. Describe your relationship with each of your parents. For each parent, answer these questions:

- What is your fondest memory?

- What is one thing about your relationship you wish you could change?

- What is the biggest impact your dad had on you? your mom?

Dad:

Mom:

5. Describe the emotions you are feeling toward each of your parents right now.

Dad:

Mom:

6. If you feel you are holding something against either or both of your parents, write a statement of how you feel, and then confess any bitterness, unresolved anger, or resentment to God as sin.

Answer question 7 if either or both of your parents are still living.

7. What is one action you need to take regarding your parents?

Peers (Option B)

1. Describe the impact that your peers had on your self-esteem for…

good:

bad:

2. As you were growing up, what value system did most of your peers hold?

3. What influence would you say your peers had on who you are today? In what specific ways?

4. Looking at your past relationships with peers, are there any incidents that you need to put behind you or people you need to forgive to put the past in perspective (see Philippians 3:13-14)?

5. How do your peers today continue to challenge your values and convictions…
positively:

negatively:

6. What, if any, peer relationships do you have that cause you to conform to wrong values and thus not fulfill

God's standard for you (see Romans 12:1-2)? If you are in a situation like this, what do you need to do about it?

The Past in General (Option C)

1. What is one significant experience, or who is one person, from your past that has shaped your self-esteem (for good or for bad)?

2. What incidents or areas from the past continue to affect you today?

3. What is one thing from this session you can use to help you deal with the past?

4. What are some practical ways your mate can help you move beyond the past?

5. Review the Scripture passages from Blueprints questions 7-9 of this session. What from these verses speaks to you? How can the message be applied in your life?

6. What are some ways you and your mate can help one another when issues from the past come up in your marriage?

Interact as a Couple [30 minutes]

1. Get together with your mate and go through each other's project. Don't condemn. Seek to understand where your mate is coming from. Be an active listener.

2. Share with your mate how you felt as you worked through the questions about the past.

3. What is something your mate can do to help you follow through with any decisions or commitments you made during this project?

4. Finish by praying with and for your mate. Look up 1 John 1:9, 2 Corinthians 5:17, and 2 Corinthians 5:21. Pray these verses back to God. Claim them as true in your life.

Remember to bring your calendar to the next session so you can Make a Date.

Planting Positive Words

The words you speak to your mate have the potential to build up or tear down your mate's self-esteem.

W A R M • U P   15   M I N U T E S

Guess Who

On a piece of paper or index card, list three or four words or phrases that describe you, then give your list to the leader. Once all the lists are turned in, the leader will, in random order, read the lists to the group. After each description is read, write your guess about who in the group the list is describing. After all the lists have been read, share your guesses, and then answer the following question:

- In what way do words have the power to paint pictures in our mind?

Project Report

Share one thing you learned from last session's Home-Builders Project.

BLUEPRINTS · · · · · · · · · · · 6o MINUTES

The Power of Words

If you have a large group, form smaller groups of about six people to answer the Blueprints questions. Unless otherwise noted, answer the questions in your subgroup. After finishing each section, take time for subgroups to share their answers with the whole group.

1. "Sticks and stones may break my bones, but words will never hurt me." As you look at this childhood statement as an adult, how do you feel about it?

2. Think about the power of words in your life. What were some statements, either positive or negative, that you heard about yourself when you were growing up that you still remember?

3. What is easier for you to recall—positive or negative words? Why?

4. Words can be compared to seeds. Negative words can cause seeds to become weeds in a person's self-esteem, while positive words can bear fruit. As a couple, look up one of the following verses and discuss what Proverbs has to say about the power of words.

- Proverbs 11:9
- Proverbs 12:25
- Proverbs 15:4
- Proverbs 16:24
- Proverbs 24:26
- Proverbs 25:11

After you and your mate have read and discussed your verse, share your verse and insights with the group.

5. Of the shared Proverbs verses, what truth most stood out to you and why?

The Power of Praise

Since words must be used carefully and constructively to build self-esteem, let's consider how best to speak rightly to your mate.

6. What is one of the best compliments or words of encouragement you have received?

7. Why do you think some people find it hard to give or receive praise? Which is harder for you to do?

8. For what character qualities can you give your mate praise?

Answer question 9 with your mate. After answering, you may want to share an appropriate insight or discovery with the group.

9. It is important to praise your mate specifically. Complete the following statements about your mate:

• Thank you for...

• You made me feel loved when...

• I like being with you because...

- I appreciate you because...

- I admire you for...

- I feel confident that you can...

- One thing that you are really good at is...

10. Read Ruth 2:2-17. What impact do you think Boaz's kind actions and words had on Ruth's self-esteem? Likewise, how do you think Boaz was affected by Ruth's kind words?

11. The pleasant exchange of words between Boaz and Ruth happened under ordinary daily circumstances as they both went about their work. In what way does their interaction challenge you to look at how you relate to your mate, especially the words you use, on a day-to-day basis?

12. As a group, brainstorm about creative ways to build-up or praise one's mate and list them.

HomeBuilders Principle:
Generous praise can transform your mate and improve your marriage.

W R A P • U P   15   M I N U T E S

Leader: See pp. 138-139 of the Leader's Notes for details about the paper cutout.

Form circles of no more than six people, with each circle having a paper cutout of a person. Pass the paper cutout around the circle. When the cutout comes to you, recall to the group a putdown of some sort, then tear off a piece of the paper person and pass the cutout to the next person. After the cutout has been around your group at least once, stop and read Ephesians 4:29.

Now pass around the paper cutout again, but this time share a complimentary or affirming word and use tape to repair the paper person. After the pieces have been re-attached to your cutout, answer the following questions:

- How was this experience like what we do to people in real life?
- Compare what happened to the paper person to what happens to real people.

Make a Date

Make a date with your mate to meet before the next session to complete the HomeBuilders Project. At the next session, your leader will ask you to share one thing from this experience.

DATE
_____

TIME
_____

LOCATION
_____

HOMEBUILDERS PROJECT   6 0   M I N U T E S

As a Couple [10 minutes]

To start your date, see if you can compliment each other all the way through the alphabet! For example, start with the letter A, and take turns saying something to your mate such as, "You're the apple of my eye," or "You're athletic," or "I admire you." Then go on to the letter B, trying to make it all the way through the alphabet. If you make it through once, you may want to try for a second time.

Individually [20 minutes]

1. What insight, discovery, or reminder from this session did you find most helpful?

2. Recall some of the words you used to affirm your mate during your courtship. How did those words affect your mate, your relationship, and you?

3. Why do you think there seems to be a tendency to become callous or insensitive to the effects words have on your mate after you've been married awhile? How can understanding the power of words begin to change the vocabulary you use with your mate?

4. What are some words from your mate that encourage you and lift your spirit?

5. What are some words from your mate that bring you down and discourage you?

6. How can you more regularly communicate praise to your mate?

Interact as a Couple [30 minutes]
1. Share with one another your answers to questions 1 through 4 in the previous section. Be open, kind, and understanding toward one another.

2. Agree on any action steps you should take and how they will be implemented.

3. Read your sentence completions to your mate. Be gracious in receiving your mate's praise and affirmation.

4. Close by praying together, thanking God for your mate.

Remember to bring your calendar to the next session so you can Make a Date.

Freedom to Fail

Learn to separate self-worth from performance by giving yourself and your mate the freedom to fail.

W A R M • U P   15   M I N U T E S

Big Dreams

Choose one of the following questions to answer and share with the group:

- What is one of the riskiest things you have ever done or tried?
- What is one thing you dream of trying if you knew you couldn't fail and if money were not an issue?
- What is a failure in your life you are able to look back at and appreciate in some way?

Project Report

Share one thing you learned from last session's Home-Builders Project.

If you have a large group, form smaller groups of about six people to answer the Blueprints questions. Unless otherwise noted, answer the questions in your subgroup. After finishing each section, take time for subgroups to share their answers with the whole group.

Failure is inevitable in life. No one ever "does it right" every time. Our mates can give us perspective and help us confront a challenge or deal with painful times— whether we lose our keys or our job.

Failure can be divided into two categories:
• Failure that is sin (such as lying, lust, or greed).
• Failure that is not sin (such as honest mistakes, misunderstandings, or forgetting things).

While all sin is failure, not all failure is sin.

During this session, we will look at the impact of sin and some steps you can use to help each other deal with failure. The primary question is, "How do you respond when your mate faces failure?"

The Impact of Failure

1. What is a failure you experienced when you were growing up that sticks with you today?

2. How did your family view failure? How does that viewpoint affect you today?

3. As a culture, we have developed a "success syndrome" that creates the mirage that only a person who is healthy, wealthy, and powerful has worth and value. What do the following Scriptures say about this philosophy?

- 1 Samuel 16:7

- Matthew 6:33

4. What is a failure you have experienced in your marriage?

Answer questions 4 and 5 with your mate. After answering, you may want to share an appropriate insight or discovery with the group.

5. What effect has this had on your marriage?

Six Steps to Giving Your Mate the Freedom to Fail

During the remainder of this session we will look at six steps you and your mate can use to give each other the freedom to risk failure and the strength to recover from it.

For Extra Impact: As the group reads the story of the prodigal son, assign these parts to readers: narrator, the younger son, the father, and the older brother.

Step One: *Offer forgiveness and restoration.* Read Luke 15:11-32.

6. From the story of the prodigal son, what can we tell about:

• the son's feelings of worth in the midst of his own failure?

• the father's response to his son's humility and desire for restoration?

7. What does this parable illustrate about God's love and acceptance of you? What does the story teach you about responding when your mate fails?

Step Two: *Assure your mate of your commitment, loyalty, and love regardless of performance.*
Read 1 John 4:18.

8. How can feeling assured of your mate's love help you when you are going through a difficult time?

Step Three: *Remind your mate, "Your worth is not in what you do but in who you are."*
Read Ephesians 1:13-14.

9. How can a person fail without being a failure? How can you send a clear "You are not a failure!" message when your mate fails?

Step Four: *Comfort your mate with the truth that God is in control.*
Read Romans 8:28.

10. Share an incident in which God brought good out of one of your failures.

Step Five: *Join with your mate in giving thanks in all things.*
Read 1 Thessalonians 5:18.

11. Why should we thank God even amidst our failures?

Step Six: *Encourage your mate not to lose heart when facing failure.*
Read 2 Corinthians 4:16-18.

12. How can your mate best encourage you during difficult times?

HomeBuilders Principle:
When you give your mate the freedom to fail, failure can become a tutor rather than a judge.

Read the following scenarios, and discuss how the steps you looked at in Blueprints could be applied to these situations.

- Howard is habitually late. He's late to work, late coming home, and late to church. What can Howard's wife do to help him?

- Sue has a great idea for a business but lacks the confidence to move beyond the idea. What can Sue's husband do to help her?

- Tom just lost his job when his company down-sized. What can Tom's wife do to help him?

- Mary freezes when it comes to making decisions. She tries to avoid situations in which she has to decide quickly. What can Mary's husband do to help her?

Make a Date

Make a date with your mate to meet before the next session to complete the HomeBuilders Project. At the next session, your leader will ask you to share one thing from this experience.

DATE

TIME

LOCATION

HOMEBUILDERS PROJECT

6 0   M I N U T E S

As a Couple [10 minutes]

Take a minute to share the following with each other:

- The one thing you remember most wanting to do or be when you grew up.

- As you grew up, what either encouraged you or discouraged you from achieving your dreams?

- What is one dream you have now—no matter how far-fetched—that you think you would like to do or try someday?

Individually [20 minutes]

1. Look through the Blueprints section, and name one important idea or technique you learned.

2. Which of the six steps studied in this session does your mate do best? Give an example.

3. Which of the steps do you need to put into action more often to help your mate?

4. In your life right now, how willing do you feel you are to take risks, despite the fear of failure? Evaluate your current "risk factor" on a scale of 1 (not willing to risk) to 10 (willing to risk freely). What ranking did you give yourself, and why?

5. Where do you fear failing the most? Circle the top two.

- at work
- as a husband or wife
- as a parent
- managing finances
- managing the household
- in a new venture
- as a friend
- emotionally
- as a Christian
- other: _____

6. Look over the six steps that follow. Place a star by the ones you feel you need the most from your mate.

1) Forgiveness and restoration.

2) Assurance of commitment, loyalty, and love regardless of performance.

3) Reminders that "My worth is not in what I do, but in who I am."

4) Being comforted with the truth that God is in control.

5) Joining your mate in giving thanks in all things.

6) Encouraging your mate not to lose heart when he or she faces failure.

Under each starred step, write a practical way your mate could meet this need for you.

Interact as a Couple [30 minutes]

1. Go through the questions from the individual section together.

2. How can you make your marriage a safe place in which each of you can risk failure?

3. Together read 1 Peter 4:8. What perspective does this verse give you on your mate's failures?

4. Pray together. Thank God for giving you the freedom to fail. Thank God that, by the power of the Holy Spirit, you and your mate can give each other the same freedom.

Remember to bring your calendar to the next session so you can Make a Date.

Keeping Life Manageable

Experience peace and balance in your marriage as you help each other follow God's priorities.

W A R M • U P   15   M I N U T E S

A Piece of the Pie

Use the diagram on the next page to make a pie chart of your "typical" day. Assign times for the following activities:

- sleeping
- eating (including preparation time)
- driving
- working
- television
- Bible study/prayer

- chores (such as paying bills, doing laundry, taking out the trash, and running errands)
- time with your mate
- time with children
- exercise
- internet
- other:_____

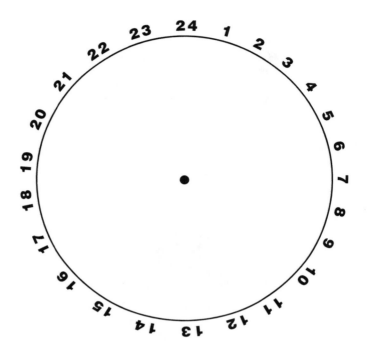

After charting your typical day, answer these questions:

- What priorities does your schedule reflect?
- Which areas in your life generally lose out to other things?

Project Report

Share one thing you learned from the last session's HomeBuilders Project.

It is impossible to avoid stress completely—stress is a part of life. But it is possible to reduce stress by making good choices about your life together as a couple. In this session, we will look at Ephesians 5:15-21, which presents three keys for making good choices.

If you have a large group, form smaller groups of about six people to answer the Blueprints questions. Unless otherwise noted, answer the questions in your subgroup. After finishing each section, take time for subgroups to share their answers with the whole group.

Stress and Self-Esteem

1. From the following list, what three factors cause the most stress for you?

- procrastination
- being overcommitted
- job demands
- change
- conflict with a child or parent
- conflict with mate
- financial pressures
- unexpected problems
- recurring interpersonal friction
- uncertain future
- health problems
- in-laws
- friends
- church involvement
- my own unrealistic expectations
- cultural pressures
- other: _____

Compare lists with your mate. Then, if you are comfortable doing so, share with the group the area of your life in which you are feeling the most stress right now.

2. How does extra stress in your life affect your self-esteem? How does it affect your marriage?

3. Is stress always a bad thing? Why or why not?

Be Wise

Your real priorities are revealed by the choices you make each day. These choices are a reflection of your true values. Your calendar and checkbook are two significant indicators of your priorities—and your values.

One of the shortcomings of couples today is that they do not take the necessary time to discuss values as a couple. A couple's priorities will be a reflection of their real values.

4. Read Ephesians 5:15-17. What does this passage

teach us about being wise in determining our priorities? How can these principles help you handle stress?

5. Read James 1:5-6. How can you more fully take advantage of what God offers here?

6. Look at the pie chart you made during Warm-Up. What changes could you make in your schedule to reduce stress in your life?

Live by the Spirit

Ephesians 5:18 exhorts us to "be filled with the Spirit," which means allowing the Spirit to direct and empower us.

7. Read John 14:26-27 and Galatians 5:16-23. What do these verses tell you about the difference the Holy Spirit can make in our lives and with what results?

8. How do you think the work of the Holy Spirit in a person's life affects his or her self-esteem? Explain.

9. Read Philippians 4:6-7. What role can prayer play in relieving stress in your life?

Complete question 10 with your mate. After doing this, you may want to share an appropriate insight or discovery with the group.

10. Together, take two or three minutes to list some specific causes of pressure in your life or marriage right now. Then, remembering the promise of Philippians 4:6-7, take a few minutes together to apply this verse directly in your lives. Pray for those situations that are causing stress and anxiety in your life and marriage. Give those situations over to God, asking for wisdom as you deal with them.

HomeBuilders Principle:
Through prayer you and your mate can ask God for wisdom to handle the pressures of life. His Holy Spirit can bring discernment, direction, peace, and order to your life and marriage.

Submit to One Another

11. Read Ephesians 5:21. How can submitting to one another help you and your mate keep from becoming overcommitted or feeling too much stress?

12. How can a healthy handling of stress in your marriage help promote positive self-esteem for you and your mate?

HomeBuilders Principle:
God has given you your mate to help you find peace, direction, and balance in life.

W R A P • U P   15   M I N U T E S

At the start of this session, you made a pie chart of your typical day. Now, using the following graph, chart what you would like your typical day to look like.

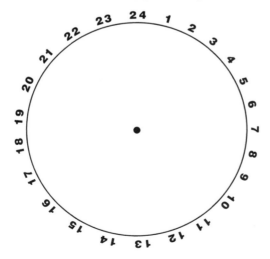

After completing your chart, answer these questions:
- What is the biggest difference between this chart and the one you did earlier?

- What is the biggest obstacle you face in trying to achieve this ideal?

Make a Date

Make a date with your mate to meet before the next session to complete the HomeBuilders Project. Your leader will ask at the next session for you to share one thing from this experience.

DATE

TIME

LOCATION

As a Couple [10 minutes]

We all need a day of refreshing now and again to help us cope with the stress of everyday living. Take a few minutes to plan the "perfect day" for your mate. Write down what this day would look like, then share what you planned for each other.

Individually [20 minutes]

1. Looking back over this session, what is the one thing you can do that would most help your mate keep life manageable?

2. Right now, what is causing stress in your life? List three to five causes, if possible.

3. What things do you think are causing the most pressure in your mate's life right now?

4. What five values do you hold as most important?

5. Look over your calendar and checkbook for the last month. What priorities and values do you feel they represent?

6. Look back at the pie charts you did in this session's Warm-Up and Wrap-Up. What about your schedule would you like to see change, and what steps do you need to take to begin this process?

7. How can your mate help you to better live the values you want your life to reflect?

Interact as a Couple [30 minutes]

1. Compare your answers from the individual section.

2. Together, list the causes of stress you noted in the individual section, categorizing them as follows:

Those We Can Control	Those We Cannot Control

3. What decisions need to be made about "Those We Can Control" so that your lives more clearly reflect your values?

4. Together, decide on some specific ways each of you can help the other maintain a balanced lifestyle. List those ideas below.

5. Read Matthew 11:28-30 together. What message do you find that relates to your lives and schedules?

6. Close your time in prayer by asking God for wisdom in helping one another keep life manageable.

Remember to bring your calendar to the next session so you can Make a Date.

Valuing Your Mate

As husband and wife, you need to love, support,
and encourage one another so that you each can
become all that God intended you to be.

W A R M • U P   15   M I N U T E S

Looking Back

As you come to the end of this study, take some time
to reflect as a group on what you have experienced.
Pick one or more of the following questions to answer
and share with the group:

- What has this group meant to you over the course
  of this study?
- What is the most valuable thing you've learned or
  discovered?
- How have you or your marriage changed as a
  result of this course?
- What would you like to see happen next for
  this group?

Project Report

Share one thing you learned from the previous session's HomeBuilders Project.

BLUEPRINTS 60 MINUTES

For this session's Blueprints, you will be in two groups—one for husbands and one for wives. The Blueprints questions for husbands start on this page; the questions for wives start on page 94.

Blueprints for Husbands

Treating Your Wife as a Participating Partner

1. Read 1 Peter 3:7. What does this verse mean to you as a husband?

2. What comes to your mind when you think of a fully participating partner?

3. List three to five ways you need your wife. Share at least one with the group.

4. Read 1 Corinthians 11:11. Why do you think it is often difficult for a man to admit his need for his wife as a partner? Under what circumstance do you find it difficult to tell your wife you need her?

5. How can showing your need for your wife build her self-esteem?

Honoring Your Wife

6. 1 Peter 3:7 exhorts the husband to "grant her honor" (New American Standard Bible). What are some ways you can communicate respect and honor for your wife?

7. What are some ways husbands may communicate disrespect and lack of honor to their wives?

8. One way of honoring is to continue to "court" your wife, showing her she is important to you. Share some ideas about how you add romance to your relationship.

Loving Your Wife

9. Read Ephesians 5:22-29. What do you think it means for a husband to love his wife "just as Christ loved the church"?

10. Ephesians 5:29 speaks of a man's responsibility to "feed" and "care" for his wife. What are some ways a husband can feed and care for his wife in the following areas?

- spiritual growth

- gifts, talents, and abilities

- dreams and visions for the future

Your Marriage Mission

11. How does respecting and encouraging your wife

bring value to her? How does this respect and encouragement benefit you and your marriage as well?

12. Organizations use mission statements to evaluate and plan the direction of their efforts. If you were to have a mission statement for yourself as a husband, what would you like it to say? Answer the following questions individually to help you develop a personal mission statement for valuing your wife.

- Up to this point, what has been your major purpose and direction as a husband?

- Looking forward, what would you like to see be your major purpose and direction as a husband?

After answering these questions, draft a one- or two-sentence mission statement.

HomeBuilders Principle:
As a husband, you are called to love your wife and help her develop into the woman God made her to be.

Blueprints for Wives

Respecting Your Husband

1. Read Ephesians 5:33b. What does it mean to respect your husband?

2. Why do you think your husband needs your respect? How is it essential to his self-esteem?

3. What are some ways you can demonstrate or communicate respect for your husband when...
- you feel he is being unreasonable?
- you disagree with a decision he has made?
- you are frustrated by his lack of participation or interest in dealing with an issue?
- you feel he doesn't give you a chance to participate in family decisions?

Submitting to Your Husband

Perhaps no other word receives as negative a response from women today as "submit." However, I believe submission is a key element of what the Bible teaches about a wife's relationship with her husband.

4. Read Ephesians 5:22-27. What does this passage say about the responsibility of a wife and the responsiblity of a husband?

5. Why do women struggle with being submissive to their husbands?

6. How would being submissive to your husband most help his self-esteem?

Understanding Your Husband

7. One major source of misunderstanding in a marriage is the difference between men and women. How is your husband different from you? For the following, jot down some of the differences between you and your mate.

Area	Me	My Husband
ways of thinking		
approach to physical intimacy		
style of communicating		
approach to problems		
background		
methods of handling conflict		
approach to managing money		

After noting differences, answer this question:

- In what area did you feel you were most different from your husband?

8. What are some ways your marriage has benefited because of the differences between you and your husband?

9. What connection do you see between your husband's work and his self-esteem?

10. Read 1 Corinthians 11:11. How does this passage compare to what our culture teaches about dependence and independence in marriage? How has this issue affected the way you relate to your husband?

Your Marriage Mission

11. How does respecting and encouraging your husband bring value to him? In what way do you and your marriage benefit from this as well?

12. Organizations use mission statements to evaluate and plan the direction of their efforts. If you were to have a mission statement for yourself as a wife, what would you like it to say? Answer the following questions individually to help you in developing a personal mission statement for valuing your husband.

- Up to this point, what has been your major purpose and direction as a wife?

- Looking forward, what would you like to see be your major purpose and direction as a wife?

After answering these questions, draft a one- or two-sentence mission statement.

HomeBuilders Principle:
A wife that loves and respects her husband will help him develop into the man God made him to be.

W R A P • U P   15   M I N U T E S

Get together with your mate and share with one another the mission statement you worked on in the Blueprints section. Then work together to draft a one- or two-sentence mission statement for your marriage. Keep in mind your statement does not mean that you have already "arrived"; rather, it is simply a statement of what you desire your marriage to become.

After drafting your marriage mission statement, pray as a couple asking God to help you to achieve the purpose he would have for your marriage.

If you're comfortable doing it, share your statement with the group.

Make a Date

Make a date with your mate to meet in the next week to complete the last HomeBuilders Project of this study.

DATE

TIME

LOCATION

HOMEBUILDERS PROJECT   6 o   M I N U T E S

As a Couple [10 minutes]
Congratulations—you've made it to the last project for this study! To start this date, reflect on how this study has affected your marriage by answering these questions:

- Thinking back to the first meeting of this study, how did you feel? What expectations did you have of this course? How did your experience compare to your expectations?

- What is something from this study that has helped your marriage?

- What is something new you learned about your mate?

- What has been the best part of this study for you?

Individually [20 minutes]

1. List at least five positive character qualities that you respect and admire in your mate.

2. What are some of your mate's talents and strengths?

3. What are your mate's dreams and goals? List as many as you can think of.

4. How can you best encourage your mate to achieve these goals?

5. Read Philippians 2:1-4. What does this passage say to you about how you are to value you mate?

6. Looking back over the session, what action do you most need to follow up on?

7. Consider the personal mission statement you wrote for valuing your mate. What is a specific action you can take to carry out this mission?

8. Close by praying for your mate. Ask God to show you what it truly means to value your mate.

Interact as a Couple [30 minutes]
1. Share with each other your answers from the individual section.

2. Considering the marriage mission statement you wrote as a part of the session, what specific action can you take together to carry out your mission?

3. Evaluate some things you might do together to continue building your marriage, as well as build up one another and others. One thing you may want to consider is continuing the practice of regularly setting aside time as you have for these projects. You may also want to look at some ideas on page 107 in "Where Do You Go From Here?"

4. Close with a time of prayer, thanking God for each other and for your marriage—what he has done and will do!

For Extra Impact

Imagine you have just received the following letter from your mate. How would you respond in writing? Use a separate sheet of paper, and write your response. (Be specific as you express how you feel.)

RSVP: This exercise is something you and your mate may want to do now or save for a later date.

My dearest husband/wife,

Thank you for choosing me to share your life. Thank you for your honesty and transparency. I know it can be painful at times.

Deep down inside, I really know that you love me. But I need tangible reminders of your love. There is very little in this life of greater value to me than your love. I need it. I need you.

Could I ask a favor? I love to receive letters from you, but I don't ever want to ask for them…it takes all the fun out of receiving them if it's my idea. But would you write me a letter?

I need to know:
- *how you appreciate me…*
- *what I've done to show that I respect you…*
- *how I've been an encouragement to you…*
- *that you appreciate the "little things" I do every week for you…*
- *that I have your unconditional acceptance, just as I am (Is it there? I need to know.)…*
- *how I am a partner with you…*
- *what you like about me…*
- *how I've changed for the better or ways that you've seen me grow (I forget sometimes)…*
- *that you want to lead me and do what is best for me…*
- *that you want to meet my friends…*

You can write it any way you'd like, but please tell me. I really do respect you.

I love you,

Your husband/wife

P.S. I'm not perfect either, but I'm glad we're in this thing together.

Where Do You Go From Here?

It is our prayer that you have benefited greatly from this study in the HomeBuilders Couples Series. We hope that your marriage will continue to grow as you both submit your lives to Jesus Christ and build according to his blueprints.

We also hope that you will begin reaching out to strengthen other marriages in your community and local church. Your church needs couples like you who are committed to building Christian marriages. A favorite World War II story illustrates this point very clearly.

The year was 1940. The French Army had just collapsed under Hitler's onslaught. The Dutch had folded, overwhelmed by the Nazi regime. The Belgians had surrendered. And the British Army was trapped on the coast of France in the channel port of Dunkirk.

Two hundred and twenty thousand of Britain's finest young men seemed doomed to die, turning the English Channel red with their blood. The Fuehrer's troops, only miles away in the hills of France, didn't realize how close to victory they actually were.

Any rescue seemed feeble and futile in the time remaining. A "thin" British Navy—"the professionals"—told King George VI that at best they could save 17,000 troops. The House of Commons was warned to prepare for "hard and heavy tidings."

Politicians were paralyzed. The king was powerless. And the Allies could only watch as spectators from a distance. Then as the doom of the British Army seemed imminent, a strange fleet appeared on the horizon of the English Channel—the wildest assortment of boats perhaps ever assembled in history.

Trawlers, tugs, scows, fishing sloops, lifeboats, pleasure craft, smacks and coasters, sailboats, even the London fire-brigade flotilla. *Each ship was manned by civilian volunteers—English fathers sailing to rescue Britain's exhausted, bleeding sons.*

William Manchester writes in his epic novel, *The Last Lion*, that even today what happened in 1940 in less than twenty-four hours seems like a miracle—not only were all of the British soldiers rescued, but 118,000 other Allied troops as well.

Today the Christian home is much like those troops at Dunkirk. Pressured, trapped, and demoralized, it needs help. Your help. The Christian community may be much like England—we stand waiting for politicians, professionals, even for our pastors to step in and save the family. But the problem is much larger than all of those combined can solve.

With the highest divorce rate of any nation on earth, we need an all-out effort by men and women "sailing" to rescue the exhausted and wounded family casualties. We need an outreach effort by common couples with faith in an uncommon God. For too long, married couples within the church have abdicated the privilege and responsibility of influencing others to those in full-time vocational ministry.

Possibly this study has indeed been used to "light the torch" of your spiritual lives. Perhaps it was already burning, and this provided more fuel. Regardless, may we challenge you to invest your lives in others?

You and other couples around the world can team together to build thousands of marriages and families. By starting a HomeBuilders group, you will not only strengthen other marriages; you will also see your marriage grow as you share these principles with others.

Will You Join Us in "Touching Lives...Changing Families"?

The following are some practical ways you can make a difference in families today:

1. Gather a group of four to eight couples, and lead them through the seven sessions of this HomeBuilders study, *Building Your Mate's Self-Esteem.* (Why not consider challenging others in your church or community to form additional HomeBuilders groups?)

2. Commit to continue marriage building by doing another course in the HomeBuilders Couples Series.

3. An excellent outreach tool is the film *"JESUS,"* which is available on video. For more information, contact FamilyLife at 1-800-FL-TODAY.

4. Host a dinner party. Invite families from your neighborhood to your home, and as a couple share your faith in Christ.

5. Reach out and share the love of Christ with neighborhood children.

6. If you have attended the FamilyLife Marriage Conference, why not offer to assist your pastor in counseling couples engaged to be married, using the material you received?

For more information about any of the above ministry opportunities, contact your local church, or write:

> **FamilyLife**
> P.O. Box 8220
> Little Rock, AR 72221-8220
> 1-800-FL-TODAY
> **www.familylife.com**

Our Problems, God's Answers

Every couple eventually has to deal with problems in marriage. Communication problems. Money problems. Difficulties with sexual intimacy. These issues are important to cultivating a strong, loving relationship with your spouse. The HomeBuilders Couples Series is designed to help you strengthen your marriage in many of these critical areas.

Part One: The Big Problem

One basic problem is at the heart of every other problem in every marriage, and it's a problem we can't help you fix. No matter how hard you try, this is one problem that is too big for you to deal with on your own.

The problem is separation from God. If you want to experience marriage the way it was designed to be, you need a vital relationship with the God who created you and offers you the power to live a life of joy and purpose.

And what separates us from God is one more problem—sin. Most of us have assumed throughout our lives that the term "sin" refers to a list of bad habits that everyone agrees are wrong. We try to deal with our sin problem by working hard to become better people. We read books to learn how to control our anger, or we resolve to stop cheating on our taxes.

But in our hearts, we know our sin problem runs much deeper than a list of bad habits. All of us have rebelled against God. We have ignored him and have decided to run our own lives in a way that makes sense to us. The Bible says that the God who created us wants us to follow his plan for our lives. But because of our sin problem, we think our ideas and plans are better than his.

- *"For all have sinned and fall short of the glory of God"* (Romans 3:23).

What does it mean to "fall short of the glory of God"? It means that none of us has trusted and treasured God the way we should. We have sought to satisfy ourselves with other things and have treated those things as more valuable than God. We have gone our own way. According to the Bible, we have to pay a penalty for our sin. We cannot simply do things the way we choose and hope it will all be OK with God. Following our own plan leads to our destruction.

- *"There is a way that seems right to a man, but in the end it leads to death"* (Proverbs 14:12).
- *"For the wages of sin is death"* (Romans 6:23a).

The penalty for sin is that we are forever separated from God's love. God is holy, and we are sinful. No matter how hard we try, we cannot come up with some plan, like living a good life or even trying to do what the Bible says, and hope that we can avoid the penalty.

God's Solution to Sin

Thankfully God has a way to solve our dilemma. He became a man through the person of Jesus Christ. He lived a holy life, in perfect obedience to God's plan. He also willingly died on a cross to pay our penalty for sin. Then he proved that he is more powerful than sin or death by rising from the dead. He alone has the power to overrule the penalty for our sin.

- *"Jesus answered, 'I am the way and the truth and the life. No one comes to the Father except through me' "* (John 14:6).

- *"But God demonstrates his own love for us in this: While we were still sinners, Christ died for us"* (Romans 5:8).

- *"Christ died for our sins...he was buried...he was raised on the third day according to the Scriptures...he appeared to Peter, and then to the Twelve. After that, he appeared to more than five hundred"* (1 Corinthians 15:3-6).

- *"For the wages of sin is death, but the gift of God is eternal life in Christ Jesus our Lord"* (Romans 6:23).

The death of Jesus has fixed our sin problem. He has bridged the gap between God and us. He is calling all of us to come to him and to give up our own flawed plan for how to run our lives. He wants us to trust God and his plan.

Accepting God's Solution

If you agree that you are separated from God, he is calling you to confess your sins. All of us have made messes of our lives because we have stubbornly preferred our ideas and plans over his. As a result, we deserve to be cut off from God's love and his care for us. But God has promised that if we will agree that we have rebelled against his plan for us and have messed up our lives, he will forgive us and will fix our sin problem.

- *"Yet to all who received him, to those who believed in his name, he gave the right to become children of God"* (John 1:12).

- *"For it is by grace you have been saved, through faith—and this not from yourselves, it is the gift of*

God—not by works, so that no one can boast" (Ephesians 2:8-9).

When the Bible talks about receiving Christ, it means we acknowledge that we are sinners and that we can't fix the problem ourselves. It means we turn away from our sin. And it means we trust Christ to forgive our sins and to make us the kind of people he wants us to be. It's not enough to just intellectually believe that Christ is the Son of God. We must trust in him and his plan for our lives by faith, as an act of the will.

Are things right between you and God, with him and his plan at the center of your life? Or is life spinning out of control as you seek to make your way on your own?

You can decide today to make a change. You can turn to Christ and allow him to transform your life. All you need to do is to talk to him and tell him what is stirring in your mind and in your heart. If you've never done this before, considering taking the steps listed here:

- Do you agree that you need God? Tell God.

- Have you made a mess of your life by following your own plan? Tell God.

- Do you want God to forgive you? Tell God.

- Do you believe that Jesus' death on the cross and his resurrection from the dead gave him the power to fix your sin problem and to grant you the free gift of eternal life? Tell God.

- Are you ready to acknowledge that God's plan for your life is better than any plan you could come up with? Tell God.

- Do you agree that God has the right to be the Lord and master of your life? Tell God.

"Seek the Lord while he may be found;
call on him while he is near"
(Isaiah 55:6).

Following is a suggested prayer:

Lord Jesus, I need you. Thank you for dying on the
cross for my sins. I receive you as my Savior and Lord.
Thank you for forgiving my sins and giving me eternal
life. Make me the kind of person you want me to be.

Does this prayer express the desire of your heart? If it does, pray it right now, and Christ will come into your life, as he promised.

Part Two: Living the Christian Life

For a person who is a follower of Christ—a Christian—the penalty for sin is paid in full. But the effect of sin continues throughout our lives.

- *"If we claim to be without sin, we deceive ourselves and the truth is not in us"* (1 John 1:8).

- *"For what I do is not the good I want to do; no, the evil I do not want to do—this I keep on doing"* (Romans 7:19).

The effects of sin carry over into our marriages as well. Even Christians struggle to maintain solid, God-honoring marriages. Most couples eventually realize that they can't do it on their own. But with God's help, they can succeed. The Holy Spirit can have a huge impact in the marriages of Christians who live constantly, moment by moment, under his gracious direction.

Self-Centered Christians

Many Christians struggle to live the Christian life in their own strength because they are not allowing God to control their lives. Their interests are self-directed, often resulting in failure and frustration.

- *"Brothers, I could not address you as spiritual but as worldly—mere infants in Christ. I gave you milk, not solid food, for you were not yet ready for it. Indeed, you are still not ready. You are still worldly. For since there is jealousy and quarreling among you, are you not worldly? Are you not acting like mere men?"* (1 Corinthians 3:1-3).

The self-centered Christian cannot experience the abundant and fruitful Christian life. Such people trust in their own efforts to live the Christian life: They are either uninformed about—or have forgotten—God's love, forgiveness, and power. This kind of Christian:

- has an up-and-down spiritual experience.

- cannot understand himself—he wants to do what is right, but cannot.

- fails to draw upon the power of the Holy Spirit to live the Christian life.

Some or all of the following traits may characterize the Christian who does not fully trust God:

disobedience	plagued by impure thoughts
lack of love for God and others	jealous
	worrisome
inconsistent prayer life	easily discouraged, frustrated
lack of desire for Bible study	critical
legalistic attitude	lack of purpose

Note: The individual who professes to be a Christian but who continues to practice sin should realize that he may not be a Christian at all, according to 1 John 2:3; 3:6, 9; Ephesians 5:5.

Spirit-Centered Christians

When a Christian puts Christ on the throne of his life, he yields to God's control. This Christian's interests are directed by the Holy Spirit, resulting in harmony with God's plan.

- *"But the fruit of the Spirit is love, joy, peace, patience, kindness, goodness, faithfulness, gentleness and self-control. Against such things there is no law"* (Galatians 5:22-23).

Jesus said,

- *"I have come that they may have life, and have it to the full"* (John 10:10b).

- *"I am the vine; you are the branches. If a man remains in me and I in him, he will bear much fruit; apart from me you can do nothing"* (John 15:5).

- *"But you will receive power when the Holy Spirit comes on you; and you will be my witnesses in Jerusalem, and in all Judea and Samaria, and to the ends of the earth"* (Acts 1:8).

The following traits result naturally from the Holy Spirit's work in our lives:

Christ centered	love
Holy Spirit empowered	joy
motivated to tell others about Jesus	peace
	patience
dedicated to prayer	kindness
student of God's Word	goodness
trusts God	faithfulness
obeys God	gentleness
	self-control

The degree to which these traits appear in a Christian's life and marriage depends upon the extent to which the Christian trusts the Lord with every detail of life, and upon that person's maturity in Christ. One who is only beginning to understand the ministry of the Holy Spirit should not be discouraged if he is not as fruitful as mature Christians who have known and experienced this truth for a longer period of time.

Giving God Control

Jesus promises his followers an abundant and fruitful life as they allow themselves to be directed and empowered by the Holy Spirit. As we give God control of our lives, Christ lives in and through us in the power of the Holy Spirit (John 15).

If you sincerely desire to be directed and empowered by God, you can turn your life over to the control of the Holy Spirit right now (Matthew 5:6; John 7:37-39).

First, confess your sins to God, agreeing with him that you want to turn from any past sinful patterns in your life. Thank God in faith that he has forgiven all of your sins because Christ died for you (Colossians 2:13-15; 1 John 1:9; 2:1-3; Hebrews 10:1-18).

Be sure to offer every area of your life to God (Romans 12:1-2). Consider what areas you might rather keep to yourself, and be sure you're willing to give God control in those areas.

By faith, commit yourself to living according to the Holy Spirit's guidance and power.

- *Live by the Spirit: "So I say, live by the Spirit, and you will not gratify the desires of the sinful nature. For the sinful nature desires what is contrary to the Spirit, and the Spirit what is contrary to the sinful nature. They are in conflict with each other, so that you do not do what you want"* (Galatians 5:16-17).

- *Trust in God's Promise: "This is the confidence we have in approaching God: that if we ask anything according to his will, he hears us. And if we know that he hears us—whatever we ask—we know that we have what we asked of him"* (1 John 5:14-15).

Expressing Your Faith Through Prayer

Prayer is one way of expressing your faith to God. If the prayer that follows expresses your sincere desire, consider praying the prayer or putting the thoughts into your own words:

Dear God, I need you. I acknowledge that I have been directing my own life and that, as a result, I have sinned against you. I thank you that you have forgiven my sins through Christ's death on the cross for me. I now invite Christ to take his place on the throne of my life. Take control of my life through the Holy Spirit as you promised you would if I asked in faith. I now thank you for directing my life and for empowering me through the Holy Spirit.

Walking in the Spirit

If you become aware of an area of your life (an attitude or an action) that is displeasing to God, simply confess your sin, and thank God that he has forgiven your sins on the basis of Christ's death on the cross. Accept God's love and forgiveness by faith, and continue to have fellowship with him.

If you find that you've taken back control of your life through sin—a definite act of disobedience—try this exercise, "Spiritual Breathing," as you give that control back to God.

1. **Exhale.** Confess your sin. Agree with God that you've sinned against him, and thank him for his forgiveness of it, according to 1 John 1:9 and Hebrews 10:1-25. Remember that confession involves repentance, a determination to change attitudes and actions.

2. **Inhale.** Surrender control of your life to Christ, inviting the Holy Spirit to once again take charge. Trust that he now directs and empowers you, according to the command of Galatians 5:16-17 and the promise of 1 John 5:14-15. Returning to your faith in God enables you to continue to experience God's love and forgiveness.

Revolutionizing Your Marriage

This new commitment of your life to God will enrich your marriage. Sharing with your spouse what you've committed to is a powerful step in solidifying this commitment. As you exhibit the Holy Spirit's work within you, your spouse may be drawn to make the same commitment you've made. If both of you have given control of your life to the Holy Spirit, you'll be able to help each other remain true to God, and your marriage may be revolutionized. With God in charge of your lives, life becomes an amazing adventure.

Leader's Notes

Contents

About Leading a HomeBuilders Group

What is the leader's job?

Your role is that of "facilitator"—one who encourages people to think and to discover what Scripture says, who helps group members feel comfortable, and who keeps things moving forward.

What is the best setting and time schedule for this study?

This study is designed as a small group home Bible study. However, it can be adapted for use in a Sunday school setting as well. Here are some suggestions for using this study in a small group and in a Sunday school class:

In a small group

To create a friendly and comfortable atmosphere, it is recommended that you do this study in a home setting. In many cases the couple that leads the study also serves as host to the group. Sometimes involving another couple as host is a good idea. Choose the option you believe will work best for your group, taking into account factors such as the number of couples participating and the location.

Each session is designed as a ninety-minute study, but we recommend a two-hour block of time. This will allow you to move through each part of the study at a more relaxed pace. However, be sure to keep in mind one of the cardinal rules of a small group: Good groups start *and* end on time. People's time is valuable, and your group will appreciate you being respectful of this.

In a Sunday school class

There are two important adaptations you need to make if you want to use this study in a class setting: 1) The material you cover should focus on the content from the Blueprints section of each session. Blueprints is the heart of each session and is designed to last sixty minutes. 2) Most Sunday school classes are taught in a teacher format instead of a small group format. If this study will be used in a class setting, the class should adapt to a small group dynamic. This will involve an interactive, discussion-based format and may also require a class to break into multiple smaller groups (we recommend groups of six to eight people).

What is the best size group?

We recommend from four to eight couples (including you and your spouse). If you have more people interested than you think you can accommodate, consider asking someone else to lead a second group. If you have a large group, you are encouraged at various times in the study to break into smaller subgroups. This helps you cover the material in a timely fashion and allows for optimum interaction and participation within the group.

What about refreshments?

Many groups choose to serve refreshments, which help create an environment of fellowship. If you plan on including refreshments in your study, here are a couple of suggestions: 1) For the first session (or two) you should provide the refreshments and then allow the group to be involved by having people sign up to bring them on later dates. 2) Consider starting your group with a short time of informal fellowship and refreshments (fifteen minutes), then move into the study. If couples are late, they miss only the food and don't disrupt the study. You may also want to have refreshments available at the end of your meeting to encourage fellowship; but remember, respect the group members' time by ending the study on schedule and allowing anyone who needs to leave right away the opportunity to do so gracefully.

What about child care?

Groups handle this differently depending on their needs. Here are a couple of options you may want to consider:

- Have group members be responsible for making their own arrangements.

- As a group, hire child care, and have all the kids watched in one location.

What about prayer?

An important part of a small group is prayer. However, as the leader, you need to be sensitive to the level of comfort the people in your group have toward praying in front of others. Never call on people to pray aloud if you don't know if they are comfortable doing this. There are a number of creative approaches you can take, such as modeling prayer, calling for volunteers, and letting people state their prayers in the form of finishing a sentence. A tool that is helpful in a group is a prayer list. You are encouraged to do this, but let it be someone else's ministry to the group. You should lead the prayer time, but allow another couple in the group the opportunity to create, update, and distribute prayer lists.

In closing

An excellent resource that covers leading a HomeBuilders group in greater detail is the *HomeBuilders Leader Guide* by Drew and Kit Coons. This book may be obtained at your local Christian bookstore or by contacting Group Publishing or FamilyLife.

About the Leader's Notes

The sessions in this study can be easily led without a lot of preparation time. However, accompanying Leader's Notes have been provided to assist you in preparation. The categories within the Leader's Notes are as follows:

Objectives

The purpose of the Objectives is to help focus the issues that will be presented in each session.

Notes and Tips

This section will relate any general comments about the session. This information should be viewed as ideas, helps, and suggestions. You may want to create a checklist of things you want to be sure to do in each session.

Commentary

Included in this section are notes that relate specifically to Blueprints questions. Not all Blueprints questions in each session will have accompanying commentary notes. Questions with related commentaries are designated by numbers (For example, Blueprints question 6 in Session One would correspond to number 6 in the Commentary section of Session One Leader's Notes).

Session One:
Strengthening Self-Esteem

Objectives

Marriage provides one of life's best relationships for building another's self-esteem.

In this session, couples will...

- enjoy sharing experiences from early in their marriages.

- discover the importance of marriage partners building each other's self-esteem.

- recognize unrealistic mental images of the ideal husband or wife that may have distorted their self-esteem.

- learn ways in which God's loving acceptance builds a sense of personal value in Christians.

- begin practicing building healthy self-esteem in their mate.

Notes and Tips

1. If you have not already done so, you will want to read the information in "About the Sessions" on pages 4 and 5, as well as "About Leading a HomeBuilders Group" (page 120) and "About the Leader's Notes" (page 124).

2. As part of the first session, you may want to review with the group some ground rules (page 10 in the Introduction).

3. Be sure you have a study guide for each person. You will also want to have extra Bibles and pens or pencils.

4. Because this is the first session, make a special point to tell the group about the importance of the HomeBuilders Project. Encourage each couple to "Make a Date" before the next meeting to complete the project. Mention that you will ask about this during the Warm-Up of the next session.

5. If you have a particularly large group, the Warm-Up may run fifteen to thirty minutes. If this happens, plan to try to get through Blueprints in forty-five to sixty minutes. It would be a good idea to mark the questions in Blueprints that you want to be sure to cover. If any questions are not covered during the session, suggest that group members plan on looking at those questions as a part of the HomeBuilders Project.

6. You will notice there is a call-out note at the start of Blueprints that recommends breaking into smaller groups if you have a large group. The reason for this is twofold: 1) to help facilitate discussion and participation by everyone, and 2) to help you to get through the material in the allotted time.

Similarly, Blueprints questions 5 and 10 in this session call for break-out groups. In these instances, break-out groups can look at multiple passages simultaneously, which will save time and allow group members to learn from each other.

7. This is the first session, so you may want to offer a closing prayer instead of asking others to pray aloud. Many people are uncomfortable praying in front of others, and, unless you already know your group well, it may be wise to slowly venture into various methods of prayer. Regardless of how you decide to close, you should serve as a model.

8. You may want to remind the group that, because this group is just under way, it is not too late to invite another couple to join the group. Challenge everyone to think of couples to invite to the next session.

9. Session One sets the tone for the series and builds a couple's appreciation for building one another's self-esteem. To accomplish the goals, the session must be fun and memorable. Do not allow the group to bog down in any areas of discussion or linger on anything negative.

10. A special caution: In recent years, some Christians have stated that the concept of "building self-esteem" is unbiblical. It is not the intent of this study to defend the subject of self-esteem, and it would be unwise for you to do so in your group. If anyone in the group has difficulty with this concept, you may want to suggest reading "A Word About Self-Esteem" on page 12.

Commentary

Here is some additional information about various Blueprints questions. The numbers that follow correspond to the Blueprints questions of the same numbers in the session. If you share any of these points, be sure to do so in a manner that does not stifle discussion by making you the authority with *the real answers*. Begin your comments by saying things like, "One thing I notice in this passage is…" or "I think another reason for this is…"

Notes are not included for every question. Many of the questions in this study are designed so that group members will draw from their own opinions and experiences.

6. Although it is good to have healthy self-esteem, this verse reminds us of the importance of proper personal humility.

10. You may want to point out that God's truth contrasts with the "phantom" in that it expresses what is truly real.

Attention HomeBuilders Leaders

FamilyLife invites you to register your HomeBuilders group. Your registration connects you to the HomeBuilders Leadership Network, a worldwide movement of couples who are using HomeBuilders to strengthen marriages and families in their communities. You'll receive the latest news about HomeBuilders and other ministry opportunities to help strengthen marriages and families in your community. As the HomeBuilders Leadership Network grows, we will offer additional resources such as online training, prayer requests, and chat with authors. There is no cost or obligation to register; simply go to www.homebuildersgroup.com.

Session Two:
Unconditional Acceptance

Objectives

Help your mate experience the liberating power of unconditional love.

In this session, couples will...

- discover their own need for acceptance and the importance of acceptance in building their mate's self-esteem.

- evaluate their commitment to accept their mate.

- explore two biblical components of acceptance.

- practice expressing acceptance with their mate.

Notes and Tips

1. Since this is the second session, your group members have probably warmed up a bit to each other but may not yet feel free to be completely open and honest about their relationship. Don't force the issue, but continue encouraging couples to attend and to complete their projects.

2. If someone joins the group for the first time in this session, give a brief summary of the main points of Session One. Also, be sure to introduce those who do not know each other. You may want to have each new couple answer a question from the Session One Warm-Up exercise.

3. Make sure the arrangements for refreshments (if you're planning to have them) are covered.

4. If your group has decided to use a prayer list, make sure this is covered.

5. There is a "For Extra Impact" exercise in Warm-Up that you may want to consider using in addition to, or in place of, the first Warm-Up exercise. If you choose to use the "For Extra Impact" exercise, you will need to either make a photocopy of the descriptions on the next page or write these descriptions on slips of paper. Also, if you do more than one exercise in Warm-Up, be sure to watch your time so the session stays on track.

6. If you told the group during the first session that you'd be asking them to share something they learned from the first HomeBuilders Project, be sure to ask them. This is an important opportunity for you to establish an environment of accountability.

7. For the closing prayer in this session, you may want to ask for a volunteer or two to close the group in prayer. Check ahead of time with a couple of people you think might be comfortable praying aloud.

8. There is a "For Extra Impact" exercise at the very end of this session. Bring this exercise to the group's attention, and suggest couples may want to do it in addition to the HomeBuilders Project or at a later date.

Descriptions for the "For Extra Impact" Warm-Up exercise, Who Are You?

Photocopy this list, then cut into slips for your group. If there are more than ten people in your group, break into multiple groups to do the "Who Are You?" exercise.

You are a serious motorcycle enthusiast. You have long hair and lots of tattoos. You recently became a Christian and are interested in learning what being a Christian is all about.

You are from a different country. "Home" for you is halfway around the world. You are in this country as a student. You do not speak the language well, and you are having a difficult time adjusting to the culture.

Until yesterday you struggled financially, working two jobs just to make ends meet. Today everything is different. You just found out that you have inherited a large sum of money from a distant relative.

You are a "spiritual" person. You believe in God—and you believe in just about everything else, as well. You are here to see what this Christian group is all about.

Your employer has just transferred you to this city. You expect your stuff to arrive this weekend, and you're trying to make friends quickly so you can ask for some help unloading your things.

You are a homeless person. Your world was recently turned upside down; you literally lost everything. You're not really sure why you're here. You heard these people were nice and there would be food, so you came.

You are extremely skeptical of Christianity. You believe there is a God, but you don't have much use for so-called "organized religion." In fact, the only reason you're here is as a favor to your spouse.

Congratulations! Your church has just appointed you to be the "volunteer" in charge of ministry to couples. You've come to the meeting to see how this group is going.

You have just experienced the loss of a loved one who died after an extended battle with AIDS. You are trying to deal with your grief and have come to this group looking for support.

You are a middle-aged, middle manager at a large company. At least, you *were*. You received notice that the company, for which you have worked since graduation, is letting you go. You're not sure what you're going to do next.

Commentary

Note: The numbers here correspond to the Blueprints questions of the same numbers in the session.

2. People want others to like them; thus they often don't have enough confidence to stand up to rejection. For many, this lack of confidence stems from a childhood in which they never felt accepted.

4. Avoidance, masks, lack of communication, keeping others at arm's length, performance to earn approval, and conformity are a variety of ways people try to protect themselves.

5. God loved us when we were still sinful. God raised us up with Christ and seated us with him in the heavenly places. God wants to show us the mercy and riches of his grace.

6. Adam knew God and trusted his provision.

9. Experiencing the kind of love described in 1 Corinthians 13 enables a person to be honest and transparent, not fearing that the other person will rebuff open communication or use what is shared later as a weapon.

Session Three:
Putting the Past in Perspective

Objectives

Build hope and gain perspective by understanding what effect the past can have on your mate's self-esteem today.

In this session, couples will...

- evaluate their own attitude about failures in the past as compared with God's Word.

- explore the proper way of looking back and living today.

- examine the power of forgiveness.

- practice God's forgiveness in their own lives and toward their mates.

Notes and Tips

1. This session focuses on hope for liberty from the past. Perhaps no other session in this study is more delicate and potentially threatening than this one. Most newlyweds have no appreciation of how much the events of their past can influence their marriage. The potential for both good and harm in this session must be recognized, and the session should be approached carefully and in prayer.

Regardless of what may have happened in a person's past, it is important to deal with this subject in a manner that's both frank and sensitive during the Bible study. While people need to confront their past honestly, no one should have to share anything that would be personally embarrassing to his or her spouse or that might bring damage or harm to anyone else as a result of sharing it.

A person can move beyond the past, but guilt and condemnation must be dealt with first. Forgiveness must be experienced vertically, from God through Jesus Christ, then horizontally, with people.

2. At some point during this session, someone may ask, "How much of my past should I share with my mate?" Ideally, oneness between two people involves no secrets. Unfortunately, we do not live in an ideal world, and sometimes information from the past can be very difficult for a person to handle.

Before sharing information that could damage a relationship, one should seek wise counsel for help with evaluating whether the information should be discussed with a counselor first.

3. If you choose to use the "For Extra Impact" exercise in Warm-Up, you will need to gather various childhood objects. A stuffed toy, a doll, a toy car, a baseball card, a glove or ball, building blocks of some kind, and a coloring book or children's storybook are all things that would work well. Anything special to you from your childhood would be good also.

4. Remember the importance of starting and ending on time.

5. You may find it helpful to make some notes right after the meeting to help you evaluate how things went. Ask yourself questions such as: Did everyone participate? Is there anyone I need to make a special effort to follow up with before the next session? Asking yourself these and similar questions will help you keep focused.

6. It's important that you and your mate complete the Home-Builders Project each session as an example to the group.

Commentary

7. In Christ we are made into new creatures.

8. We must trust what God is doing now and not dwell on past defeats.

Note: The numbers here correspond to the Blueprints questions of the same numbers in the session.

9. If there are people in your group who may not be familiar with the life of the Apostle Paul, you may want to briefly share about his life. See Acts 22, 26 and 2 Corinthians 11:16-33 for details about Paul's life.

11. Obviously, we should forgive. But forgiving someone who has caused deep hurt is very difficult, if not impossible, for someone who has never experienced God's forgiveness.

Ephesians 4:32 summarizes how best to deal with offenses in our own past and to help our mate do the same. This verse calls us to deal with the others' pasts as God has dealt with our past and to initiate kind, loving actions in the present. You may want to pose the question: "Since God has been kind and loving toward you and has given up his right to punish you, how should you and your mate respond to each other's past mistakes?"

You may also want to share the following definition of forgiveness: "To forgive means to put away the right to punish another, to respond to past failures without resentment or accusation."

Session Four:
Planting Positive Words

Objectives

The words you speak to your mate have the potential to build up or tear down your mate's self-esteem.

In this session, couples will...

- examine biblical and personal insights into the power of words.

- evaluate how they express praise to their mate.

- identify praiseworthy qualities possessed by their mate.

- practice expressing praise to their mate.

Notes and Tips

1. Congratulations. With the completion of this session, you will be over halfway through this study. It's time for a checkup: How are you feeling: How is the group going? What has worked well so far? What things might you consider changing as you head into the second half?

2. This can be the most enjoyable session of the study because its focus is highly positive. Everyone enjoys being complimented. Beyond making people feel good, positive words can have a lasting impact on an individual and on a marriage. In the opposite direction, negative words can have a profoundly harmful impact.

3. For Warm-Up in this session, group members will be guessing one another's identity based on a list of descriptive words they write about themselves and that you read to the group. Tell the group that, to make this more interesting, they might want to use descriptions that may not be immediately obvious. For example, if one person in the group has red hair, that person should not use redheaded. Traits (patience), talents (tennis), or tendencies (shyness) would serve better.

You will need paper or index cards for this exercise.

4. For Wrap-Up in this session, you will need to make copies of the paper cutout on the next page. You will need at least one paper cutout for every six people in your group. To be safe, you may want to plan on having at least one more copy than you think you will need. For a sturdier cutout, you may want to make your cutouts from construction paper.

You will also need tape for each cutout. To make this exercise most effective, use masking tape.

5. By this time, group members should be getting more comfortable with each other. For prayer at the end of this session, you may want to give everyone an opportunity to pray by asking the group to finish a sentence that goes something like this: "Lord, I want to thank you for ..." Be sensitive to anyone who may not feel comfortable doing this.

For best results, enlarge this page by 150-175%. Also, be sure to read note number 4 on the opposite page.

6. You and your mate may want to write notes of thanks and encouragement this week to the couples in your group. Thank them for their commitment and contribution to the group, and let them know that you are praying for them. (Make a point to pray for them as you write the note.)

Commentary

Note: The numbers here correspond to the Blueprints questions of the same numbers in the session.

1. For many people the reality is words hurt much more than "sticks and stones."

7. People can find it hard to give praise for several reasons: for example, if they have rarely received it, they may not know how; they may feel they should praise others sparingly so their position of authority and power is strengthened; or they may find it easier to poke fun or playfully disagree than to express affirmation and support. The last example may be a habit for a person who has good intentions but simply does not feel comfortable directly expressing a positive emotion.

People can find it hard to receive praise if they sense the attitude of the person giving praise is not one of honest appreciation. When attitude and actions are not in tune, they sense they are being flattered or manipulated.

Session Five:
Freedom to Fail

Objectives

Learn to separate self-worth from performance by giving yourself and your mate the freedom to fail.

In this session, couples will...

- express situations in which they failed in the past.

- examine failure and its effects.

- explore the biblical perspective on true success.

- consider specific steps to encourage in their mate the freedom to risk failure.

Notes and Tips

1. In this session, you deal with the subject of failure. It might be wise to remind group members not to share anything that would embarrass their mate.

2. If you feel that there are people in your group who may be struggling with overcoming past failure due to sin, you may want to mention the article in the back of their books (p. 109), "Our Problems, God's Answers." They can read it on their own and may find it helpful.

3. As the leader of a small group, one of the best things you can do for your group is to pray specifically for each group member.

Why not take some time to pray as you prepare for this session?

4. For Wrap-Up in this session, you might find it helpful to have group members first jot down some responses to the various scenarios that are presented and then share and discuss.

Commentary

Note: The numbers here correspond to the Blueprints questions of the same numbers in the session.

3. 1 Samuel 16:7: God looks at the heart, not the outer appearance.

Matthew 6:33: God's kingdom is the foundation upon which any good thing in life must be built.

If we are going to learn to handle failure and the risk of failure, we must start from the understanding that true success in life is often very different from the surface trappings of success that tend to consume so much of our physical and emotional energy.

6. The prodigal: He felt unworthy to be a son.
The father: He was full of compassion and forgiveness.

7. God is always ready to forgive and restore; we should be willing to do the same.

8. This assurance can give you greater freedom to risk failure.

Session Six:
Keeping Life Manageable

Objectives

Experience peace and balance in your marriage as you help each other follow God's priorities.

In this session, couples will...

- disclose factors that contribute to stress for them and their mate.

- examine biblical principles for determining priorities and handling pressure.

- consider how the Holy Spirit enables a person to handle the stresses of life successfully.

- pray as a couple about dealing with specific stresses of life.

Notes and Tips

1. In Warm-Up, the group is charting a "typical" day. If anyone is having trouble figuring out what a "typical" day is, suggest charting the previous day.

2. *Looking ahead:* For Blueprints in Session Seven, husbands and wives will be in two different groups. For this part of the study, you will need to have a person lead the group you're not in. Be sure to make arrangements for this ahead of time. Your mate may be a good choice for this.

3. *Looking ahead (part two):* For the next session—the last session of this study—you may want to have someone, or a couple, share what this study or group has meant to him or her. If this is something you think would be good, be thinking about who you will ask to share.

Commentary

Note: The numbers here correspond to the Blueprints questions of the same numbers in the session.

2. A person who feels overwhelmed by stress is not likely to maintain positive self-esteem. Effectively managing stress builds a person's sense of value.

3. Stress can be good if it helps you keep your priorities straight and if it helps you trust God with your life. It can be bad if it causes problems in your work, family, and relationship with God.

4. We should be wise in the way that we live, making the most of our time and turning away from what is foolish and toward what God would have us do.

8. The love, joy, and peace that are evident in our lives when we are directed by the Holy Spirit inevitably affects self-esteem.

11. One way would be to agree that you and your mate will check with each other before accepting a commitment. This agreement would provide a time and thought buffer, as well as inviting the other person's feedback in the decision.

Session Seven:
Valuing Your Mate

Objectives

As husband and wife, you need to love, support, and encourage one another so that you each can become all that God intended you to be.

In this session, husbands and wives will...

- develop personal mission statements for valuing their mate.

- affirm their need for their mate.

- discuss the importance of understanding, respecting, and encouraging their mate.

- work together to develop a mission statement for their marriage.

Notes and Tips

1. While this HomeBuilders Couples Series has great value, people are likely to gradually return to previous patterns of living unless they commit to a plan for carrying on the progress made. During this final session of the course, encourage couples to take specific steps beyond this series to keep their marriages growing. For example, you may want to challenge couples who developed the habit of a "date night" during the course of this study to continue this practice. Also, you may want the group to consider doing another study from this series.

2. Session Seven is unique because husbands and wives will meet in separate groups for the Blueprints section in this session. Providing separate environments for men and women should facilitate a more open discussion of issues related to how they value their mates.

Be sure to arrange for two comfortable rooms where the groups can meet and not disturb each other.

3. Be sure to allow enough time for the last question in Blueprints (both for husbands and for wives) because it becomes a point of discussion between husbands and wives in Wrap-Up.

4. The "For Extra Impact" exercise at the very end of this session is something you can bring to the group's attention as an exercise couples may want to do later, in addition to the HomeBuilders Project.

5. As a part of this, the last session, you may want to consider devoting some time to plan for one more meeting—a party to celebrate the completion of this study!

Commentary

Blueprints for Husbands

Note: The numbers here correspond to the Blueprints questions of the same numbers in the session.

Note: In preparing for this session, be sure you have reviewed points 2 and 3 in the preceding Notes and Tips.

1. Husbands should regard their wives as full partners in their lives.

2. Many men keep their wives at a distance and do not let them into the interior of their lives. A person can feel like a full partner only when there is full, open disclosure.

4. Most men are raised to believe they should be self-reliant. A man's ego often makes it difficult for him to admit that he has a need for anyone.

5. A person's sense of value is strongly influenced by knowing that he or she matters to someone.

9. To love your wife "just as Christ loved the church" involves loving your wife with complete humility, sacrificing for her, and regarding her needs as more important than your own.

Blueprints for Wives

Note: In preparing for this session, be sure you have reviewed points 2 and 3 in the preceding Notes and Tips.

Note: The numbers here correspond to the Blueprints questions of the same numbers in the session.

1. To respect your husband means to value him, to give him honor, and to build him up and praise him for what he does well. It means to let him know he is significant and important.

2. Only by receiving respect from the most important person in his life is a man enabled to grow into a more "respectable" husband.

4. Many Christian husbands and wives do not realize that, when Scripture presents the concept of submission, it puts that concept in a radical context. Immediately after calling for wives to submit to their husbands, Paul instructs husbands to love their wives "as Christ loved the church." Therefore, while the Bible does give husbands responsibility for leading the home, it also tells them to do so with an attitude of complete humility, sacrificing for their wives and considering their wives' needs as more important than their own.

10. One factor that has contributed to tensions between men and women is the cultural pressure that pushes wives to become independent of their husbands. This cultural message conflicts with this passage. Husbands and wives need each other.

Notes

Prayer Requests

Notes

Prayer Requests

Notes

Prayer Requests

Notes

Prayer Requests

Exciting Resources for Your Adult Ministry!

The Dirt on Learning
Thom & Joani Schultz

This thought-provoking book explores what Jesus' Parable of the Sower says about effective teaching *and* learning. Readers will rethink the Christian education methods used in their churches and consider what really works. Use the video training kit to challenge and inspire your entire ministry team and set a practical course of action for Christian education methods that really *work!*

ISBN 0-7644-2088-7   Book Only
ISBN 0-7644-2152-2   Video Training Kit

The Family-Friendly Church
Ben Freudenburg with Rick Lawrence

Discover how certain programming can often short-circuit your church's ability to truly strengthen families—and what you can do about it! You'll get practical ideas and suggestions featuring profiles of real churches. It also includes thought-provoking application work-sheets that will help you apply the principles and insights to your own church.

ISBN 0-7644-2048-8

Disciple-Making Teachers
Josh Hunt with Dr. Larry Mays

This clear, practical guide equips teachers of adult classes to have impact—and produce disciples eager for spiritual growth and ministry. You get a Bible-based, proven process that's achieved results in churches like yours—and comes highly recommended by Christian leaders like Dr. Bruce Wilkinson, Findley Edge, and Robert Coleman. Discover what needs to happen before class through preparation, in class during teaching, and after class in service to turn your adult classes into disciple groups.

ISBN 0-7644-2031-3

Extraordinary Results From Ordinary Teachers
Michael D. Warden

Now both professional *and* volunteer Christian educators can teach as Jesus taught! You'll explore the teaching style and methods of Jesus and get clear and informed ways to deepen your teaching and increase your impact! This is an essential resource for every teacher, youth worker, or pastor.

ISBN 0-7644-2013-5

Discover our full line of children's, youth, and adult ministry resources at your local Christian bookstore, or write: Group Publishing, P.O. Box 485, Loveland, CO 80539. www.grouppublishing.com

Since attending a FamilyLife Marriage Conference, the Martins' love really shows...

But who's keeping score?

FamilyLife Marriage Conference
Get away for a "Weekend to Remember"!

Chalk one up for your marriage! Get away to a FamilyLife Marriage Conference for a fun, meaningful weekend together. Learn how to understand your mate, build your marriage, and much more.

To register or receive more information,
visit www.familylife.com or call 1-800-FL-TODAY.

FAMILYLIFE™
Bringing Timeless Principles Home

"FamilyLife Today" radio programs have...

Principles to help strengthen your marriage and ways to love your mate from your

Soul

Advice for parents of both preschoolers and adolescents—it's sure to help Mom and

Pop

Practical, biblical teaching to build your home on Christ, the true

ROCK

Insights from Dennis Rainey and Bob Lepine on a wide variety of family issues—lots of good

Talk

"FamilyLife Today"—A great format for your family!

Call your favorite local Christian radio station for broadcast times and start listening today!

FAMILYLIFE
T·O·D·A·Y™

Make Your Marriage the Best It Can Be!

Great marriages don't just happen—husbands and wives need to nurture them. They need to make their marriage relationship a priority.

That's where the **newly revised** HomeBuilders Couples Series® can help! The series consists of interactive 6- to 7-week small group studies that make it *easy* for couples to really open up with each other. The result is fun, non-threatening interactions that build stronger Christ-centered relationships between spouses—*and* with other couples!

Whether you've been married for years, or are newly married, this series will help you and your spouse discover timeless principles from God's Word that you can apply to your marriage and make it the best it can be!

ISBN 0-7644-2249-9

The HomeBuilders Leader Guide gives you all the information and encouragement you need to start and lead a dynamic HomeBuilders small group.

The HomeBuilders Couples Series® includes these life-changing studies:
HomeBuilders Leader Guide
Building Teamwork in Your Marriage
Building Your Marriage
Building Your Mate's Self-Esteem
Growing Together in Christ
Improving Communication in Your Marriage
Making Your Remarriage Last
Mastering Money in Your Marriage
Overcoming Stress in Your Marriage
Raising Children of Faith
Resolving Conflict in Your Marriage

FAMILYLIFE™
Bringing Timeless Principles Home
www.familylife.com

Look for the **HomeBuilders Couples Series**® at your local Christian bookstore or write:

P.O. Box 485, Loveland, CO 80539
www.grouppublishing.com